BIBLICAL FOUNDATIONS FOR THE ECONOMIC WAY OF THINKING

Teacher's Guide

© 2016 INSTITUTE FOR FAITH, WORK & ECONOMICS.

■ ■ ■

All rights reserved. No part of this book may be used or reproduced by any means, graphic, electronic, or mechanical, including photocopying, recording, taping or by any information storage retrieval system without the written permission of the publisher except in the case of brief quotations embodied in critical articles and reviews. The views expressed in this work are solely those of the author. Because of the dynamic nature of the Internet, any web addresses or links contained in this book may have changed since publication and may no longer be valid.

All rights reserved.
9780997536911

Published by
The Institute for Faith, Work & Economics
8400 Westpark Drive
Suite 100
McLean, Virginia 22102

www.tifwe.org

INTRODUCTION

Dear Parents and Teachers,

First, thank you for using *Biblical Foundations for the Economic Way of Thinking* with your children and students. We believe that the powerful, biblical content of this course will be formative to the future of students who use it. We are grateful that you chose this elective out of so many options. We hope and pray the content of this course reaches beyond each student. You may find the biblical principles and practical solutions in this course valuable in your own life!

This grading rubric and teacher's guide are meant to serve as a guideline. The goal of this course is to encourage students' thoughtful reflection and eager engagement with the materials. That will look different for every student, so please use your discretion and judgment as necessary. This guide includes the course introduction, the syllabus, a summary of each module, suggested answers to study questions, and the answer keys to the midterm and final exams.

We hope these tools are valuable for you, and we value your feedback. Please let us know what you liked about the course materials, what you did not like, what you would change, and how your student enjoyed the course so that we may continue improving our materials. You can reach us at info@tifwe.org.

In Christ,
The Institute for Faith, Work & Economics

CONTENTS

Introduction 1

Course Introduction 5

Syllabus 7

Module Summaries 13

Study Questions 17

Midterm Answer Key 35

Final Exam Answer Key 43

About the Institute for Faith, Work & Economics 49

COURSE INTRODUCTION

The *Biblical Foundations for the Economic Way of Thinking* course is a seventeen-week high school homeschool elective course. The course guides students through an in-depth, biblical exploration of the economic way of thinking.

Students will learn the basic principles of economics. What makes IFWE's course unique is its emphasis on learning the biblical foundations for economics as a necessary component of making God-honoring decisions.

Using a variety of readings, students will learn how thinking economically can provide a framework for living that fits God's design, brings him glory, and allows them to experience fulfillment in their lives.

When God created the world, he designed us to cultivate the flourishing of his creation and glorify him in the process. To do this, he equipped each of us with unique gifts and skills we are to use to "be fruitful and multiply and fill the earth" (Gen. 1:28). This command in Genesis is a call to stewardship. In a world of limited time and resources, we need to make good decisions in order to be faithful stewards of all God gives us.

The economic way of thinking is a tool God has given us to make decisions that fit with his design and glorify him as well as serve others.

By gaining an understanding of economics, students will learn how to make wise decisions while living under conditions of scarcity and limited knowledge. They will learn the importance of being able to freely exchange their time, abilities, and resources with others in order to produce more prosperity than they could on their own. They will gain discernment as they learn about trade-offs and opportunity costs, things that will help them make wise use of their time and create value using their unique gifts and talents.

In short, students who take this course will see how living out biblical economic principles empowers them to live faithfully as Christians, to flourish and to contribute to the flourishing of their families, their communities, their nation, and, ultimately, the world.

COURSE REQUIREMENTS

1. There is one book required for the course:
   a. Gwartney, James D., Richard L. Stroup, and Dwight R. Lee. *Common Sense Economics: What Everyone Should Know about Wealth and Prosperity.* New York: St. Martin's Press, 2005.
   a. There are also numerous readings and educational videos that can be found online at http://homeschool.tifwe.org.
2. A midterm and final exam will be given to help students think reflectively about the material and their own understanding of the economic way of thinking. These exams are worth 25 percent of the student's total grade each, and the discussion questions count for fifty percent.

COURSE OBJECTIVES

After completing this course, students should:

- Understand the economic way of thinking as a path to better stewardship
- Grasp the importance of good decision-making for serving God and his creation
- Understand the grounding of economic thinking in biblical principles
- Be provoked to always ask "Why?" and "At what cost?" when evaluating different economic paths

COURSE LAYOUT

Each module consists of several sections designed to guide students comprehensively through the material. Modules begin with a brief **description** of content and review of the previous material. **Learning objectives** state the main idea for the module's content. **Key ideas** highlight important concepts not to be missed in each lesson. **Scripture readings** note all Scripture references for the introductory material. **Reading assignments** list required and optional readings for related content. **Study questions** are designed to ensure reading comprehension and encourage reflection. **Assessments**, if listed, explain writing assignments designed to apply concepts presented in the material to the students' own lives. Group or family **learning activities** offer suggested group exercises to further apply and examine important concepts. A **summary** wraps up the module and prepares students for the next lesson.

SYLLABUS

The links to reading assignments that can be found online are available at http://homeschool.tifwe.org. However, if you are accessing this book on a computer, you can access them by clicking the readings' links.

MODULE 1—GOD'S DESIGN AND DESIRE: THE PURPOSE OF ECONOMICS
1. Genesis 1–4
2. Brian Baugus, "Can Genesis Teach Us Anything about Economics?"
3. Art Lindsley, "The Call to Creativity"
4. Jonathan Pennington, "A Biblical Theology of Human Flourishing"
5. Hugh Whelchel, "Four Principles of Biblical Stewardship"
6. Hugh Whelchel, "Carrying Out the Cultural Mandate Is Essential for Biblical Flourishing"
7. Shawn Ritenour, "An Unexpected Source of Human Flourishing"
8. Econ Free, "Economic Freedom and the Quality of Life" (video)
9. IFWE, "Freedom to Flourish" (video)

MODULE 2—SELF-INTEREST AND GOD-HONORING DECISIONS
1. Art Lindsley, "C. S. Lewis, Greed, and Self-Interest"
2. Samuel Gregg, "Self Interest, Rightly Understood"
3. Anne Bradley, "Goldman Sachs, Self-Interest, and Greed"
4. Hugh Whelchel, "What Is Biblical Self-Interest?"
5. Jay W. Richards, "Selfishness, Self-Interest, and Significance"
6. Aeon J. Skoble, "Libertarian Philosophy: Why Thieves Hate Free Markets" (video)
7. Milton Friedman, "Greed" (video)

MODULE 3—THE FOUNDATIONAL IDEAS OF ECONOMICS
1. James D. Gwartney, Richard L. Stroup, and Dwight R. Lee, *Common Sense Economics*, Part 1
2. Leonard E. Read, "I, Pencil"
3. Anne R. Bradley, "You Can Spend Six Months and $1,500 Making a Chicken Sandwich…but Should You?"
4. Adam Smith, *The Wealth of Nations*, Book 1, Chapters 1–4
5. Donald J. Boudreaux, "Comparative Advantage"
6. Russell Roberts, "Incentives Matter"
7. Steven Horwitz, "Economists and Scarcity: The Concepts of 'Scarcity' and 'Resources' Are Often Misunderstood"
8. IFWE, "I, Smartphone" (video)
9. Tyler Cowen, "Introduction to Microeconomics" (video)

MODULE 4—THE ROLE OF TRADE IN HUMAN FLOURISHING
1. Russell Roberts, "Treasure Island: The Power of Trade, Part I: The Seemingly Simple Story of Comparative Advantage"
2. Russell Roberts, "Treasure Island: The Power of Trade, Part II: How Trade Transforms Our Standard of Living"
3. R. Mark Isaac, "Does the Bible Condemn Trade?"
4. David R. Henderson, "Opportunity Cost"
5. David R. Henderson, "TANSTAAFL, There Ain't No Such Thing as a Free Lunch"
6. Hugh Whelchel, "What Are the Economic Implications of the Fall?"
7. Art Carden, "Trade Is Made of Win, Part 1: Wealth Creation" (video)
8. Thomas Sowell, "There are No Solutions, Only Tradeoffs" (video)

MODULE 5—DECENTRALIZED KNOWLEDGE, PROPERTY RIGHTS, AND PRICES
1. Friedrich August von Hayek, "The Use of Knowledge in Society"
2. Art Lindsley, "Private Property"
3. Walter Kaiser, "Ownership and Property in the Old Testament Economy"
4. Russell Roberts, "Where Do Prices Come From?"
5. Donald J. Boudreaux, "Information and Prices"
6. Shawn Ritenour, "Three Reasons Private Property Is Essential for Human Flourishing"

MODULE 6—THE MARKET PROCESS, SUBJECTIVE VALUE, AND UNPLANNED ORDER
1. Max Borders, "Subjective Value"
2. Brian Baugus, "How Does the Market Work?"
3. Russell Roberts, "The Reality of Markets"
4. Anne Bradley, "The Market Process and the Path to Flourishing"
5. Russell Roberts, "A Marvel of Cooperation: How Order Emerges without a Conscious Planner"
6. Friedrich August von Hayek, "Kinds of Order in Society"
7. Anne Bradley, "Is the Economy a Pie?"
8. Hans Rosling, "200 Countries, 200 Years, 4 Minutes" (video)
9. Tom J. Bell, "Can Order Be Unplanned?" (video)
10. Donald J. Boudreaux, "Subjective Value" (video)
11. Steven Horwitz, "Spontaneous Order and the Market Process" (video)

MODULE 7—PRICES, PROPERTY RIGHTS, AND PROFITS

1. David R. Henderson, "Demand"
2. Robert Sirico, "Why Profits are Not Exploitative"
3. Armen A. Alchien, "Property Rights"
4. Robert Sirico, "Prices Keep Profits Fair"
5. Anne Bradley, "Making a Profit: An Unexpected Way to Help Others"
6. Michael Munger, "They Clapped: Can Price-Gouging Laws Prohibit Scarcity?"
7. Alex Tabarrok, "The Demand Curve" (video)
8. Alex Tabarrok, "The Supply Curve" (video)
9. Alex Tabarrok, "The Equilibrium Price" (video)
10. Tyler Cowen, "A Deeper Look at the Demand Curve" (video)
11. Tyler Cowen, "The Demand Curve Shifts" (video)
12. Alex Tabarrok, "A Deeper Look at the Supply Curve" (video)
13. Marginal Revolution University, "The Supply Curve Shifts" (video)
14. Alex Tabarrok, "Exploring Equilibrium" (video)

MODULE 8—ECONOMIC FREEDOM AND STEWARDSHIP

1. James D. Gwartney, Richard L. Stroup, and Dwight R. Lee, *Common Sense Economics*, Parts 2 and 3
2. Alan S. Blinder, "Free Trade"
3. Anne Bradley and Joseph Connors, "Economic Freedom and the Path to Flourishing"
4. Anne Bradley, "Five Reasons Christians Should Embrace Economic Freedom"
5. Econ Free, "Episode One: Economic Freedom and Quality of Life" (video)
6. Econ Free, "Episode Two: Economic Freedom in America Today" (video)

MODULE 9—ENTREPRENEURSHIP AND INNOVATION

1. Ludwig von Mises, "Profit and Loss"
2. Wolfgang Kasper, "Competition"
3. Brian Baugus, "Entrepreneurship within a Biblical Worldview"
4. Elise Daniel, "Meet the Generation Bringing Back Entrepreneurship in America"

MODULE 10—MIDTERM

MODULE 11—ECONOMIC FREEDOM AND THE DEVELOPING WORLD
1. Sara Corbett, "Can the Cell Phone Help End Global Poverty?"
2. Laurence Chandy and Geoffrey Gertz, "With Little Notice, Globalization Reduced Poverty"
3. Robert E. Lucas Jr., "The Industrial Revolution: Past and Future"
4. Derek Thompson, "The Economic History of the Last 2,000 Years: Part II"
5. Tolu Ogunlesi and Stephanie Busari, "Seven Ways Mobile Phones Have Changed Lives in Africa"
6. The World Bank, "Mobile Phone Access Reaches Three Quarters of the Planet's Population"
7. Hans Rosling, "200 Years, 200 Countries, 4 Minutes" (video)
8. Hans Rosling, "Hans Rosling and the Magic Washing Machine" (video)
9. Donald J. Boudreaux, "The Hockey Stick of Human Prosperity" (video)

MODULE 12—THE ROOTS OF POVERTY
1. Jonathan Pennington, "'Sell Your Possessions and Give to the Poor': A Theological Reflection on Jesus' Teaching Regarding Personal Wealth and Charity"
2. Theology of Work Project, "God's Law Calls People of Means to Provide Economic Opportunities for the Poor"
3. Glenn Sunshine, "Who are the Rich and the Poor?"
4. Art Lindsley, "Five Myths about Jubilee"
5. Theology of Work Project, "Productive Opportunities for the Poor"

MODULE 13—THE ROLE OF ECONOMIC FREEDOM IN ALLEVIATING POVERTY
1. Kristine Zambito, "When It Comes to Alleviating Poverty, Here's How Your Church Can Avoid Help that Hurts"
2. Steven Horwitz, "Contemporary Economic Myths"
3. Elise Daniel, "Economic Freedom is Not Enough for Human Flourishing"
4. Robert A. Lawson, "Economic Freedom"
5. Anne Bradley, "Freedom and Flourishing"
6. Jeffrey Dorfman, "Free Markets Unquestionably Help the Poor"
7. IFWE, "Flourishing" (video)

MODULE 14—GOVERNMENT AND THE ECONOMY
1. J. P. Moreland, "A Biblical Case for Limited Government"
2. Robert P. Murphy, "The Costs of Government"
3. Donald J. Boudreaux, "Free Trade and Globalization: More than Just 'Stuff'"
4. Robert Higgs, "Government Growth"
5. James Madison, "Federalist #10"

MODULE 15—GOVERNMENT AND UNINTENDED CONSEQUENCES

1. Frédéric Bastiat, *The Law*
2. Frédéric Bastiat, "What Is Seen and What Is Not Seen"
3. Anne Bradley, "Does the Minimum Wage Hurt the People It's Trying to Help?"
4. Brian Griffiths, "Christianity, Socialism, and Wealth Creation"
5. Antony Davies, "Unintended Consequences of Price Controls" (video)
6. Alex Tabarrok, "Price Ceilings" (video)
7. Alex Tabarrok, "Price Ceilings: Rent Controls" (video)
8. Alex Tabarrok, "Price Floors: The Minimum Wage" (video)
9. Alex Tabarrok, "Price Floors: Airline Fares" (video)

MODULE 16 – FINAL REFLECTIONS

1. Peter J. Boettke, *The Battle of Ideas: Economics and the Struggle for a Better World*
2. Art Lindsley, "The Biblical View of Freedom"
3. EconStories, "'Fear the Boom and the Bust' Hayek vs. Keynes Rap Anthem" (video)

MODULE 17—FINAL EXAM

MODULE SUMMARIES

MODULE 1: GOD'S DESIGN AND DESIRE: THE PURPOSE OF ECONOMICS
This module will help you understand how economics is part of God's created order and not the "dismal science" it is known to be. God's design for his creation is that it glorifies him and flourishes. We are called to work and exercise creativity, and when we do these things and make God-pleasing decisions, God is glorified. We are also able to bring about greater flourishing in creation. In this process, economics helps us become better decision makers.

MODULE 2: SELF-INTEREST AND GOD-HONORING DECISIONS
Self-interest is part of how God designed us. As his sub-creators, he made us to always be improving and innovating. When we pursue our self-interest in a biblical manner within the framework of good decisions that glorify God, we bring about greater levels of flourishing. When we pursue our self-interest by putting ourselves ahead of Christ, God's desires are not fulfilled. Self-interest is the biblical mechanism of human choice. It is motivated by our subjective value, what we want and desire – which must be Christ-centered in order for us to contribute to and experience greater flourishing.

MODULE 3: THE FOUNDATIONAL IDEAS OF ECONOMICS
The economic way of thinking helps us to understand that we are a part of a much bigger story. None of our work occurs in a vacuum. Let's say your summer job is working at a store. You may be asked to clean the floors and refill the paper towels. These jobs aren't there just for you to earn a paycheck. The store owner pays you to do these things because it's cheaper for you to do it than for him or her to do it. Our work is interconnected with the work of others, and it is incumbent upon us to figure out who God made us to be so that we can do our work well and serve as many people as possible. These ideas are known as comparative advantage and specialization, and they are the cornerstone of trading activity. They rest upon making good decisions within the framework of God's design and desires. When we do even the smallest jobs well, we contribute to our own flourishing and the flourishing of others.

MODULE 4: THE ROLE OF TRADE IN HUMAN FLOURISHING
We are limited and finite. That is why we need to be in a community and trade with others. We can't possibly produce everything we rely upon to thrive. Think of all the things you rely on every day and how difficult it would be if you had to produce them all on your own. Not only are we limited in our gifts, but we are unique in our desires as well. This is subjective value. We each prefer different kinds of music, art, colors, and styles. These unique desires change depending on time, our circumstances, our needs, new knowledge, etc. Different people desire different things. This means that people will want to trade for different things to meet different desires and will often value the same thing differently.

MODULE 5: DECENTRALIZED KNOWLEDGE, PROPERTY RIGHTS, AND PRICES

As humans we have imperfect, limited knowledge. This makes it harder to overcome our conditions of scarcity and lower our relative opportunity costs. Because we don't possess all the knowledge we need to make God-honoring decisions, we must find ways to collect, harness, and simplify knowledge. Knowledge is decentralized, local, and often "man on the street." The knowledge necessary to run or plan an economy does not exist in one place and is not available to one mind. The question of flourishing makes it imperative for us to have a system of trade that fosters the transfer of knowledge and economizes on what we need to know. Prices help us in this regard. They act as signals of changing underlying levels of scarcity, and they give us information that would be difficult or impossible for us to acquire in any other way.

MODULE 6: THE MARKET PROCESS, SUBJECTIVE VALUE, AND UNPLANNED ORDER

The market is a process through which individuals come together to trade with each other. This trade is driven by self-interest. This self-interest is guided by subjective value and the pursuit of improved conditions. Voluntary trade benefits both parties. We will never know how much any person gains from an individual trade because subjective value is so deeply embedded in who we are as people. We often can't articulate it, and it can change from day to day. We can assume that if we are not being forced to trade, we are gaining from the trades we make. But a trade we are willing to make today we may not make tomorrow.

MODULE 7: PRICES, PROPERTY RIGHTS, AND PROFITS

Prices and profits are important for making good decisions. Economist Peter Boettke often refers to the necessary "three P's" in economics: prices, property rights, and profits and losses.[1] Those three P's gives us the "three I's": incentives, information, and innovation. We need property rights to incentivize individuals to produce and make investments with their human and financial capital. Prices emerge through individual trade based on property rights and the ability to make contracts. These prices give individuals the information they need to assess how much they want a certain good or service based on their subjective values. Profits and losses give important information to suppliers and entrepreneurs about how well they are satisfying consumer wants and needs.

MODULE 8: ECONOMIC FREEDOM AND STEWARDSHIP

We need freedom to obey the cultural mandate and put our God-given creativity and talents to work. If God is calling you to open a small business, you need to be unencumbered by regulations and corruption to do that. The *Economic Freedom of the World Annual Report* is a way to measure the material flourishing that is possible in a society.[2] When people live in a society with economic freedom, we can say that they live in an opportunity society in which they are more free to pursue what God calls them to do.

MODULE 9: ENTREPRENEURSHIP AND INNOVATION

The cultural mandate tells us to work the garden and take care of it. This happens when we make good decisions and use our gifts to cultivate God's creation in an effort to serve others. One important way we serve others is by finding new ways of doing things. This is what entrepreneurs do. They tinker, invent, and innovate. It would be a mistake to think that the only people who do this are entrepreneurs like Bill Gates. Even in the lowliest jobs, we can better the conditions of others by finding better and cheaper ways to do our work. Entrepreneurs drive prosperity by innovating. It is God's design for us that the work of our hands can glorify him, have lasting and eternal significance, benefit us through the paycheck we receive, and fulfill the needs of others.

MODULE 10: MIDTERM

MODULE 11: ECONOMIC FREEDOM AND THE DEVELOPING WORLD

Christians have a mandate to care for the poor. Jesus ministered and cared for those who were poor, orphaned, widowed, and vulnerable. We must do the same, but good intentions are not enough. We must be good decision makers, considering both the costs and the consequences of our choices when we seek help for the poor. The best long-term and sustainable solution to poverty is to elevate the dignity of the person by enabling them to use their God-given creativity to serve others. This requires economic freedom, which will provide greater opportunities for the poor.

MODULE 12: THE ROOTS OF POVERTY

Poverty is a result of the fall of humankind into sin; God did not create humankind in a condition of poverty. It is not part of God's original design, nor is it his desire for us or his creation. In some cases, poverty is caused by our own sin, like the person who becomes addicted to drugs and loses their home. In other cases, it is caused by things outside of a person's control, such as sickness, natural disasters, or outside oppression. Spiritual poverty will always be with us. Material poverty doesn't have to be. Economics can help us bring about greater flourishing through God-honoring decision-making.

MODULE 13: THE ROLE OF ECONOMIC FREEDOM IN ALLEVIATING POVERTY

The market is an emergent process that brings people together based on their subjective values that drive human choice. The most vulnerable around the world are those that are largely exempt from the benefits that markets bring. Thus, poverty alleviation must concern itself not just with giving resources to the poor, but helping the poor to cultivate their creative gifts.

MODULE 14: GOVERNMENT AND THE ECONOMY

The government is an institution that, when operating well, can support the rule of law and protect both people and property rights. These protections provide a robust environment for economic progress, human creativity, and greater economic freedom. Government can also be an entity that takes property, violates human life, and engages in theft. Cronyism is a danger to good government—over time government can be subject to special interests and create winners and losers.

MODULE 15: GOVERNMENT AND UNINTENDED CONSEQUENCES

Our actions have immediate consequences. They can also have long-term, unintended consequences. We must consider both if we are to make God-honoring decisions. Government actions can actually hurt those they purport to help. This may not be done intentionally, but when we fail to consider the long-term effects of our actions, we don't envision some of these consequences that can come about.

MODULE 16: FINAL REFLECTIONS

In this final module, we encourage a reflection on the whole course and the specific results discerned in the previous module.

ENDNOTES:

1. "Boettke on Mises." Hosted by Russell Roberts. EconTalk. *Library of Economics and Liberty*, December 27, 2010, www.econtalk.org/archives/2010/12/boettke_on_mise.html.

2. James Gwartney, Robert Lawson, and Joshua Hall, *Economic Freedom of the World 2015 Annual Report*, with the assistance of Ryan Murphy, Hans Pitlik, Dulce M. Redín, and Martin Rode (Fraser Institute), http://www.freetheworld.com/2015/economic-freedom-of-the-world-2015.pdf.

STUDY QUESTIONS

Below you will find study questions for each module along with suggested answers. Some answers will vary based on each student's personal understanding and insight.

MODULE 1: GOD'S DESIGN AND DESIRE: THE PURPOSE OF ECONOMICS

1. When does trade and potential for trade occur in Genesis? Are we created to serve each other through our gifts?
   a. *In Genesis we begin to see that we are made uniquely and not self-sufficient.*
   b. *We see the potential for trade because we know that God created Adam and Eve differently, with unique gifts and talents. Thus, human exchange based on different talents is inevitable.*
   c. *Even in the garden with abundant resources before the Fall, there was still a need for specialization in order to create something out of something.*

2. Can we flourish alone? Why or why not?
   a. *No. It would be very difficult for us to flourish on our own, because we are limited in our gifts and finite.*
   b. *Our unique differences make it necessary for us to come together through trade to serve each other.*
   c. *We were created to be in community with one another to use our talents and creativity to bring about flourishing. Flourishing comes when we can focus on our gifts and improve them rather than trying to do everything alone.*

3. How does human nature make us interdependent?
   a. *Each person was created with a unique calling to pursue the furtherance of God's kingdom. This brings him glory.*
   b. *Producing every good that we consume by ourselves would be impossible. Because some are more productive at certain tasks than others, we can rely on each other for the production of different goods.*
   c. *Resources are distributed differently over the earth, and we must rely on one another for the provision of those resources.*
   d. *We are asked to cultivate God's creation. To do this we must come together through exchange.*

4. How can we live out the cultural mandate in different forms?
    a. *We are all called to "be fruitful and multiply" and "to subdue the earth."*
    b. *God has given each of us unique talents and gifts in order to carry out that mandate.*
    c. *Being fruitful and multiplying may mean building families, church, schools, cities, institutions, laws, etc.*
    d. *Subduing the earth may mean planting crops, building houses, innovating new technology, running a small business, etc.*

5. How does our God-given creativity help us bring about flourishing?
    a. *Our God given creativity helps us to carry out the cultural mandate, which commands us to cultivate his good creation through the application of our gifts.*
    b. *God has given each of us human creativity to be used to build, grow, and subdue the earth, and to bring about new things and expand his creations for the flourishing of his people.*

6. Can accountants, engineers, and others in "secular" occupations bring glory to God?
    a. *Yes. All of these occupations contribute to God's call for us to work in this world, and they all have the potential to bring glory to God. We see this with certainty when we discover what God has created us to do and go do it.*
    b. *God desires that we steward the gifts he has given us. If someone is gifted with a brain for engineering, God is glorified when that person stewards and uses their gift to bring about new creations in this world. In pursuing engineering, that person is serving others with those talents.*

7. What is the distinction between biblical flourishing and typical cultural definitions of flourishing?
    a. *Cultural definitions of flourishing typically encompass more individualized senses of flourishing – i.e. personal wealth, leisure time, security, etc. They also tend to focus on a secular humanist vision of whatever is good for me is good.*
    b. *The biblical definition of flourishing tells us that the idea of flourishing is innate to our human being. Human flourishing is what drives us to live in peace, love, and happiness because it results from making God-pleasing decisions.*

MODULE 2: SELF-INTEREST AND GOD-HONORING DECISIONS

1. How do you act on your self-interest in your daily life?

    Answers will vary. An example: I choose to study for a test in a class that I do not necessarily enjoy in order to gain new knowledge. Self-interest can and often does involve sacrifice. It is how we make choices. When we allow Christ to reign in our hearts, our self-interest is God-focused. This is how he created us to be. Now we can make more God-honoring decisions.

2. What are the ways that this, for you, could turn into greed?

    Answers will vary. An example: I could become very success driven in school and make receiving good grades an idol. Whenever we replace God's desires and interests with our own, then our self-interest can turn into the lust for greed and idolatry.

3. Are rich people necessarily greedy? Why or why not?

    No. Both rich and poor are capable of being greedy because it is a condition of our hearts and our priorities. Rich people could have gained their wealth from acting in self-interest that serves the common good. It might not be the result of greed. Also, the poor can lust after wealth. Being greedy does not depend on our bank accounts. It depends on the condition of our hearts.

4. How does economics help us understand how self-interest can be used to serve others?

    When a producer of a good or service acts in self-interest, they have to take into mind the needs, preferences, and values of the consumer in order to make a profit. The free market harnesses self-interest for the common good. The only way to make a profit is to consider the needs of consumers and give them the best product in both price and quality.

MODULE 3: THE FOUNDATIONAL IDEAS OF ECONOMICS

1. How can we think about biblical stewardship in the context of economics?

    God has provided us each with unique gifts and abilities. Our abilities are finite and relative. When we discover what we can do at a relatively lower cost than others, we have discovered our "comparative advantage." This will change depending on our trading partners. By stewarding our comparative advantages, we will bring about greater productivity in our homes and workplaces. Stewardship is about making God-pleasing decisions that maximize the benefit and minimize the expenditure of our time and talents. This leaves us with more leftover resources to utilize in other ways.

2. Why do we need incentives to make decisions? Can't we just rely on altruism?
    a. *Because we live in a fallen world, sin damages and complicates our desires – even altruistic desires. We also have different subjective values and thus we prefer different things. This means we are motivated by different things. To motivate someone well, you must understand their preferences.*
    b. *Incentives help us serve others by making prudent or sacrificial uses of scarce resources.*
    c. *Example: A farmer could just use all of his produce for himself. However, he is incentivized to make a profit and therefore sell his goods so others can enjoy his resources.*

3. How and why does division of labor make sense biblically and economically? What are the advantages of division of labor for the individual and society?
   a. *Division of labor makes sense economically and biblically because we understand that God has gifted each of us with individual talents. We can bring about greater levels of productivity when we divide labor based on our specialized individual skill set, or "comparative advantage." We cannot do everything all by ourselves. When we divide labor, we can specialize and become better at our gifts. This allows us to be more productive and create more value for those around us.*
   b. *When the division of labor occurs, the individual is rewarded for stewarding his/her unique gift, and society also benefits from a more productive use of scarce time and resources.*

4. Does anyone know how to make a pencil? Why does this matter?
   a. *No one person knows how to make a pencil. It is impossible for one person to harness all the knowledge required to create a pencil.*
   b. *This process requires multiply layers of resources, specialization, and trade from hundreds of thousands of dispersed individuals.*
   c. *This matters because it shows us how important trade is for productivity. Without trade, we would not have new and innovative technologies that help us to be more productive every day. We would not have simple products like the pencil, let alone more sophisticated products like smartphones and cars.*

5. What does market trade do? On what does it rely?
   a. *Market trade allows us to divide work that needs to be done based on our comparative advantage and exchange based on our needs and our subjective values. This results in greater productivity and a better use of scarce resources.*
   b. *Market trade relies on incentives (prices, profits and losses, and property rights)*

6. What is subjective value, and how is it part of God's created design? How does it affect our choices? What can change our subjective values?
   a. *Subjective value encompasses our personal preferences, which may be different than others'. We have distinct dispositions as a result of God's crafting us and so our desires our different from one another.*
   b. *Our subjective value will change as our circumstances, motivations and desires change.*

MODULE 4: THE ROLE OF TRADE IN HUMAN FLOURISHING

1. What does it mean to say that scarcity will always be with us? Why does this make economics important?
    a. *Because we live in a fallen world, scarcity will always be a part of our lives on this earth. We are limited and finite. We each have twenty-four hours in a day, and not one of us knows how many days we have on this earth to do what God has called us to do. Every minute counts.*
    b. *Until the new heavens and the new earth come with the return of Christ, we will always be facing the reality of scarce time and resources.*

2. What does it mean to think like an economist?
    To think like an economist is to understand how to be a good steward of God's creation and our talents in order to live productively in a world of scarcity. It means that we must count the costs of all of our actions, understand that nothing is "free", and look at the potential long-term consequences of our actions.

3. Apply the economic way of thinking to the following scenarios:
    a. *You are a lawyer and a parent. What would you take into consideration if you are thinking about hiring a maid?*
    b. *Consider your talents as a cleaner and the time it would take to clean the house and the time that would take out of your job as a parent or a lawyer.*

4. You can take an airplane or a bus from Washington, DC, to New York City. The plane takes one hour and costs $190. The bus takes four hours and costs $40. Which would you take if you were a lawyer? Which would you take if you were a waitress? Discuss all the factors that would go into your decision.
    a. *If you were a lawyer, you would likely take the plane and if you were a server, you would likely take the bus.*
    b. *This is because as a lawyer your time is costlier. Each hour you work as a lawyer you may make an average of $80 an hour, so each hour lost at work costs more. As a server, you may make on average $10 an hour, therefore each hour lost working costs less to you.*

5. How does the economic way of thinking allow us to overcome the economic problem of scarcity?
    Economics helps us weigh costs and benefits, and understand risks and uncertainty to make better decisions on how to use scarce resources. The economic way of thinking is about being a good steward of our time and talents because we must always try to understand what we are giving up against what we are getting in any exchange.

6. Do mutually beneficial trades always create value, even though we have the same scarce resources? Why or why not?

   Yes, mutually beneficial trades always create value. Value created may be subjective and based on individual desires, but each person is served based on their comparative advantage and subjective value in a mutually beneficial trade. This is true as long as the exchange is voluntary and God-honoring.

7. Discuss the link between opportunity cost, comparative advantage, and scarcity.

   Scarcity creates the need for humans to be conscientious about how they use their resources because we always face a tradeoff. Every choice we make entails a cost – the cost of the forgone opportunity. Our choices involve the use of scarce time and resources (e.g., spending time making dinner from fresh produce vs. picking up a quick meal at a fast-food restaurant). Understanding the opportunity cost in decision-making helps humans better understand the cost of their choices. Comparative advantage helps people understand their unique talents and gifts that allow them to be more productive at a particular activity than someone else and therefore use scarce time and resources better.

8. Why is it important to consider opportunity cost when making a decision?

   Considering opportunity cost in making a decision is important because it shows us the cost of the foregone opportunity. We will better understand how to weigh our options and understand the cost and benefits of options when we understand the cost of what we are giving up when making a decision.

MODULE 5: DECENTRALIZED KNOWLEDGE, PROPERTY RIGHTS, AND PRICES

1. What does a free-market economy mean? Which institutions are involved in a free-market economy? What is the outcome?

   A free-market economy is an economy based on voluntary economic exchange that is driven by the subjective value of individuals and relies on the relative comparative advantage of those individuals for the production of goods and services. These economies tend to see rapid technological progress through the unleashing of human creativity and entrepreneurship. This allows a high degree of material well-being and prosperity. This voluntary economic exchange is nested within the rule of law, well-defined and well-protected property rights, and freedom.

2. How do prices emerge in the free market?

   Prices emerge from consumers' subjective value and their willingness to pay for a product, which shows the individual demand a consumer places on a product. Thus, prices depend on well-defined property rights and emerge through voluntary exchange of individuals.

3. Explain what it means to say that prices serve as a resource allocation tool.

   Prices send signals to producers about the subjective value of consumers. This ensures that resources will be allocated to their highest valued use.

4. What kind of information do prices communicate to the buyers and sellers in a market?
   a. *Prices communicate to buyers the scarcity of a product and help buyers determine whether or not they value a product based on how much they are willing to pay for the product.*
   b. *Prices communicate to sellers how much a product is valued by consumers.*

5. How do prices help overcome the decentralized nature of knowledge?

   Prices respond to the supply and demand of a product and communicate information we would otherwise not know about consumer preferences. Prices act as signals about underlying levels of scarcity and often we could not gather or fully understand or process this information on our own. Prices change as underlying levels of scarcity change and in that, they send us signals (give us knowledge) about the changing levels of scarcity.

6. If prices are emergent and based on scarcity, how will we ever know if a price is "too high"?

   It would be difficult to objectively know if a price, which emerges voluntarily through trade, is too high unless no one shows up to purchase the good or service. Prices are relative and as long as economic exchange is voluntary then the willingness to pay will be different for each buyer. Buyers always want prices to be as low as possible and sellers always want to charge as much as they can, but the power is in the buyer in that they can walk away from a price they deem "too high." When buyers walk away often, the seller is induced to lower the price to something more buyers would be willing to pay.

7. What is the function of profits? Of losses? What would happen if we didn't have profits and losses?
   a. *Profits signal to the producer that their product creates value for a large group of individuals. It is a feedback mechanism that works through the price that brings together the buyers with the most willing demanders. When there is profit, we have leftover resources, whether it's our time or our talents, and then we can use these leftovers to serve others in a variety of ways. Profit is what we should all strive for.*
   b. *Losses signal to the producer that they are not putting resources to their most valued use in a variety of ways. It could be that the price is too high, that the product is not valued, or that some aspect of the product does not meet what consumers desire for that given price.*
   c. *Without profits and losses, producers would have no way of understanding the value consumers place on any given product. Profits and losses are necessary feedback mechanisms from buyers to sellers which help ensure the most prudent and productive use of our scarce resources.*

8. What incentivizes companies and individuals to supply their goods and services in the marketplace?
   The incentive for companies to supply the market with their goods and services comes from the motivation to incur profit. Profit happens when we create value in society by unleashing our creative talents in the service of others.

9. Why is it important that prices are flexible?
   Flexible prices ensure that resources will be properly allocated to their most valued use based on consumer preferences. Changing levels of scarcity mean that prices need to be able to change so that scarcity can accurately be reflected. This gives consumers an important signal as to whether they should consume more or less depending on the price movement. If prices increase for some reason, we can make adjustments to lessen our consumption. This is much easier if there are a variety of substitute goods from which we can choose. Decreasing prices are a signal of greater abundance of a particular good or service and we can consume and store more of that good.

10. What would happen to incentives without private property? What would happen to productivity? Why?
    Without private property, incentives to maintain and improve property would be lost. Productivity would be lost. This is because when an individual owns the property they are using to produce and sell resources, they are more motivated to preserve and expand that property and use it creatively to serve others by seeking a profit. Without the incentive of ownership, an individual's work on that property is vulnerable and inconsistent.

11. What inspires and results from profit and loss?
    Profit and loss inspire producers to find the best uses of their resources, usually resulting in greater productivity and the benefit of society as a whole.

MODULE 6: THE MARKET PROCESS, SUBJECTIVE VALUE, AND UNPLANNED ORDER

1. Can biblical flourishing and economic progress coexist? Why or why not?
   Yes. Because we each have individual preferences and desires, we are able to engage in voluntary trade in a way that is mutually beneficial. Market trade allows us to use the unique gifts and talents God has given us to serve one other through our comparative advantages. Economic well-being is an important aspect of biblical flourishing.

2. How does a market economy ration goods? What is the role of market trade in resource allocation?

    The market rations goods through prices. Every resource we desire to use is scarce. Thus, we must have a way to ration them, and prices help us do that. Through prices we can evaluate how much we want an item relative to how much we must give to have it. When we see an increase in scarcity, we know that there will be a price response in a market economy. Increasing scarcity drives up the price of the resource and signals to consumers to decrease demand or pull out of the market for that good, thereby rationing the resource.

3. How does the free-market system incentivize people and companies to supply goods and services to others?

    Free-markets incentivize people to supply goods and services to consumers because they offer the possibility of profit, or leftover resources. When you go to work you are offered a paycheck, and in that you are seeking to profit by having as much income leftover as possible. When you do profit, it is a sign that you are creating value for others. This is a powerful incentive for us to use our creative gifts well and identify needs in the community. Incentives through profit are the reasons for breakthrough technologies like pacemakers, GPS systems, and airbags in cars. All of these innovations are the result of human creativity finding better ways of doing things and solving problems for consumers.

4. How can we apply what we know about human nature to how people make decisions in the market? Are human nature and the function of the market compatible? If so, explain how. If not, explain the incongruities.
    a. *According to God's design, we are rational, intentional, and purposeful agents. These qualities help us make decisions in the market whereby we seek to use our gifts to cultivate God's good creation. In this, we glorify him. When we do this well, we bring about greater flourishing.*
    b. *Our knowledge and capacity to learn is finite and imperfect. The market functions to help provide us with better information through prices. Through trade we are able to have much greater levels of flourishing because we are relieved from having to produce everything alone.*
    c. *The market functions to better direct our self-interest to make decisions that will benefit us and society.*

5. How is it possible to create value if we are bound by scarcity?
    a. *All goods exist in scarce quantities.*
    b. *Every good is valued differently because each individual determines what he/she values. Resources are therefore not inherently valued but instead subjectively valued.*

6. Explain spontaneous order. How does it emerge in the market?
   a. *Spontaneous order is order that comes not as a product of design. It is an order that emerges from the bottom up through individual exchange.*
   b. *Examples are the evolution of language, law, money, and cultural norms.*
   c. *Spontaneous order arises through a process of social exchange over a long period of time. People adjust to what helps them best exchange with others, this can be formal, through the legal system, and informal, through the use of cultural norms and traditions (like shaking hands).*

7. Discuss free trade and coercion in terms of whether they can ensure mutual benefit, and why or why not.
   a. *The free market is a term to explain the voluntary exchanges between two people or a group of people (exchanging goods and services, for example).*
   b. *Voluntary exchange occurs in the free market because both parties expect to gain from the exchange.*
   c. *When we coerce two or more parties to exchange we cannot ensure that both parties are better off. In most cases, one group has lobbied for a benefit that will harm or exclude others. Coercion often results in winners and losers, whereas voluntary exchange always benefits both parties to the exchange.*

8. Imagine you have two autographed baseballs you want to sell online. When people bid, the Derek Jeter baseball reaches $1,140, but the baseball signed by your little league coach only reaches $14.50, including the bucket of baseballs that comes with it. What explains the difference in prices?
   The difference in prices between a baseball signed by Derek Jeter and a bucket of baseballs with one baseball signed by your little league coach comes from the greater value placed on the baseball signed by Derek Jeter. Because Derek Jeter is famous and there is only one of him, a baseball signed by him is highly valued. The baseball signed by Derek Jeter is scarcer than the ball signed by your little league coach.

MODULE 7: PRICES, PROPERTY RIGHTS, AND PROFITS

1. What are some factors that can shift the supply curve?

    The cost of resource prices, taxes, technological changes, and the number of sellers in a market.

2. More graphing of supply and demand:
    a. Graph the effects of an increase in income on the market for pizza.

        An increase in income could create an increase in demand for pizza if you really enjoy pizza and are now able to afford it more often.

    b. Graph an increase in the demand for peanut butter on the market for jelly.

        An increase in demand for peanut butter could create an increase in demand for jelly because peanut butter and jelly are complements.

    c. A drought hits Idaho. Graph the supply response in the market for potatoes.

        The drought would create a decrease in supply. The supply curve would shift to the left.

    d. How does supply respond when we levy a tax on gasoline used for cars? Ask students how the supply or demand curve would shift on a graph.

        Demand on gasoline would decrease resulting in a new equilibrium price and quantity.

3. What happens when something or someone who is not a market participant, such as a law or a central planner, artificially sets prices?

    Artificially setting prices in the market results in "deadweight loss". People's choices do not have as great a say in determining how products are valued. Artificially set prices distort the market.

4. Why would it cost $25 to park in downtown DC but only $2.50 to park in Houston, Texas? What do these disparities reflect? Are parking lot owners greedier in DC and more altruistic in Texas? Are there better-quality parking spots in DC?
    a. *It costs more to park in downtown DC than in Houston because the demand for parking in DC is greater than that of Houston and the supply of parking in DC is also likely less than the supply of parking in Houston.*
    b. *Parking lot owners are able to increase the prices of spots in DC because they know that people are willing to pay.*

5. If a country is faced with a bad wheat crop, would they run out of wheat? Why or why not?

    If the country is operating on a free-market system, they would not likely run out of wheat because competition would ensure that there are other wheat producers that will continue to supply wheat to the market.

6. Evaluate the validity of the following statement: When milk prices rise, it is because supply decreases and demand increases.

   That is possible but not necessarily true. If the supply of milk alone decreases, we are left with higher prices. If demand increases, that acts to increase prices even more than we had with just the supply decrease.

MODULE 8: ECONOMIC FREEDOM AND STEWARDSHIP

1. Discuss which institutions and rules of the game are driving or inhibiting the success of the top ten and bottom ten countries in terms of economic freedom, respectively.

   The five pillars of economic freedom are the following: (1) Government is small relative to the size of the economy; (2) Rule of law; (3) Freedom to trade; (4) Sound money; (5) Levels of regulation.

2. Explain how and why voluntary exchange creates value.

   Voluntary exchange creates value because people or groups of people would not come together to exchange voluntarily if they did not believe they would benefit from the exchange. People place value on resources or services subjectively, so two people may come together to exchange for items they value more than the current owner.

3. Give an example of a policy with an unintended consequence. How would economic thinking prevent it?
   a. *Rent control is a price ceiling that comes from a regulation that has the unintended consequence of stifling supply and innovation.*
   b. *Thinking like an economist could have prevented this unintended consequence because it would lead one to recognize that the free market will supply more housing if there is a profit motive to do so. Instead of putting a price ceiling in order to keep costs down, the free market allows for competition. As more producers enter the market in response to demand, supply will increase and the price will lower.*

4. Discuss the idea of the growing economic pie. Does the government create value? Why or why not?

   The economy is not really a pie because economic growth is not fixed. It has the potential to grow exponentially. The government can only provide the environment for economic freedom, but it cannot create value in the way that market exchange can through the provision of goods and services. The government must provide and enforce the rule of law.

5. If we are bound by scarcity, why are standards of living so much higher now than they were two hundred years ago, even though the resources at our disposal have not changed?

   We have found new and more productive ways to use scarce resources.

MODULE 9: ENTREPRENEURSHIP AND INNOVATION

1. Why is it that competition is a good thing, but perfect competition is not the goal?
   a. *Competition is a good thing because it creates a system where we get the most out of scarce resources.*
   b. *Perfect competition however, is not the goal because it is not possible; it is more of a textbook hypothetical example of an extreme case of competition.*

2. What does competition encourage?
   Innovation, quality improvements, lots of alternative goods, and lower prices.

3. What incentives does a company have in a competitive market? Who benefits from competition?
   A company is incentivized to provide the best quality for the lowest price. Consumers benefit most from competition.

4. What is the role of the entrepreneur in bringing about more freedom for others? How does this happen?
   Entrepreneurs have the ability to recognize demand and find new and innovative ways to meet that demand. This is extremely difficult but it is done best when they live in a society with a great deal of economic freedom.

5. Name three ways one can be an entrepreneur.
   a. *Taking risks*
   b. *Creative approach to an old way of doing something*
   c. *Using skills to impact the world*

MODULE 10: MIDTERM

Answers to the midterm exam questions are in the next section.

MODULE 11: ECONOMIC FREEDOM AND THE DEVELOPING WORLD

1. What changed around 1700 to cause the hockey stick of economic growth?
   The Industrial Revolution caused a great deal of innovation, global trade, and sound economic institutions, which propelled entrepreneurship and unleashed human creativity.

2. How does demand for high-tech cell phones in the US encourage cell phone use in developing countries?

   The demand for high-tech cell phones in the US has provided those in developing countries with more productive ways of carrying out their business. This makes their business more profitable so that they can continue to afford and use a cell phone. The old cell phones that most will not use in the first world have become so cheap to produce that they are in high demand in the third world and more accessible to the world's poor. These phones save time and increase their productivity.

3. Explain how the Industrial Revolution has been a process of global coordination and service.
   a. *The Industrial Revolution created an increase in the division of labor and allowed people to specialize in areas where they had comparative advantage.*
   b. *With increased division of labor and specialization, countries can focus on areas of the market where they have comparative advantage and collaborate globally through trade to exchange goods and services throughout the world.*

4. What made the Industrial Revolution different in terms of the spread of global trade?

   The Industrial Revolution allowed for the spread of global trade by freeing people up from the tasks keeping them from being more productive (like collecting water) to allow them to focus on increasing their specialized skills.

5. What are the biggest threats to economic freedom in the United States today? What can Christians do to affect this in the future?
   a. *Threats to economic freedom in America come in the form of social welfare programs that make the poor dependent on the government instead of being free to flourish; increasing levels of regulation that make it harder for entrepreneurs to open businesses; and fiscal debt that burdens society and future generations.*
   b. *Christians need to be more mindful of economic freedom and what is at stake in the United States. We must ask how we can better empower the poor to live into their gifts and vocations, cut back excessive regulations, and stop spending at such high national levels.*

6. Consider a country like Pakistan, one of the most destitute places on the planet. What would it take to get greater levels of economic freedom, private property rights, rule of law, and generally good institutions there?
   a. *The country would need to embrace free market economics to industrialize and allow for greater competition in the production of goods and services.*
   b. *The government would need to take seriously the rule of law (i.e. property rights, justice in the courts, freedom to start a business, etc.) in creating greater opportunities for economic development.*

MODULE 12: THE ROOTS OF POVERTY

1. What does the life of Jesus teach us about wealth and charity?
    a. *Wealth is not evil in itself, but it becomes evil when it is accumulated based on greed or used to oppress others. Money should never be loved or sought after more than God.*
    b. *While we are not all called to literally sell all our possessions and give to the poor, Jesus still commands that we care for those in need by using the gifts and wealth we are given to serve the poor. We do this by recognizing them as people, respecting their God-given dignity, giving them the help they need, and helping them cultivate their gifts.*

2. What does it mean to say that we should want to "help the poor help themselves"?
    We should seek to help the poor develop skills in order to sustain themselves economically. This phrase is similar to the "teach a man to fish and you feed him for a lifetime" saying.

3. What is the gospel solution to poverty? Give an example of how this solution worked in the Bible.
    We must care for the poor, but we must recognize that many of the world's poor have the potential to support themselves if they can utilize their gifts. We must form relationships with the poor in order to be able to help them best.

4. List two responsibilities of the church toward the poor, two responsibilities of the rich toward the poor, and two responsibilities of the poor.
    a. *Responsibilities of the church toward the poor: provide opportunities for the poor to overcome their poverty; be a leader in economic thought and generosity.*
    b. *Responsibilities of the rich toward the poor: providing the vulnerable with productive work; protect the rights of the poor.*
    c. *Responsibilities of the poor: avoid a lazy/sloth-like attitude; try to find productive work.*

5. List the five myths of Jubilee.
    a. *Jubilee is not meant for the forgiveness of debt.*
    b. *Jubilee involves redistribution of wealth (land).*
    c. *Jubilee shows the relative nature of private property.*
    d. *Jubilee leads to income equality.*
    e. *Jubilee is a universally applicable principal.*

MODULE 13: THE ROLE OF ECONOMIC FREEDOM IN ALLEVIATING POVERTY

1. Is the market a force against poverty? Why or why not?

   The market is a force that helps fight against poverty by increasing access to goods and services needed for economic growth.

2. By discussing their definition and their impact, explain how wealth redistribution and wealth creation are different. What are the implications of each for societal flourishing?
   a. *Wealth redistribution does not create new value. Exchange in wealth redistribution is not voluntary, so it often falls short of the true needs of the poor and stifles societal flourishing.*
   b. *Wealth creation improves lives by providing better options for improved quality of life.*

3. Explain how progressive cheapening happens and what effects result from it.
   a. *Progressive cheapening is the process by which producers create a new technology that spreads from the rich to the masses.*
   b. *When the new technology is first introduced, the cost is very expensive. This high cost allows producers to carry out research and development in order to find ways to make the product less expensive.*
   c. *Now we can get a lot more for our money.*

4. How can the church get involved in poverty alleviation? List practical applications from this chapter on programs churches can implement to truly help the poor.
   a. *Three broad ways of helping the poor are relief, rehabilitation, and development.*
   b. *The church can start a relief program that sends aid to a country that has just been hit by disaster.*
   c. *The church can start a rehabilitation program that directly involves local community members in the rehabilitation of a neighborhood distorted by war. The key in this is that members of the local community are leaders in the project.*

5. For the poor, what are the tangible benefits of increased access to markets for the poor?

   Increased access to the market provides the poor with better options and improved quality of life.

MODULE 14: GOVERNMENT AND THE ECONOMY

1. Explain how wealth redistribution and wealth creation differ by discussing their definitions and their impact. What are the implications of each for societal flourishing?
   a. *Wealth redistribution does not create new value. Exchange in wealth redistribution is not voluntary, so it often falls short of the true needs of the poor and stifles societal flourishing.*
   b. *Wealth creation improves lives by providing better options for improved quality of life.*

2. Does the government provision of goods/services work to the short-term or long-term advantage of the poor?

   The government's provision of goods/services may provide the poor with short-term advantages, but in the long-term government provision of goods/services can have a harmful effect on the poor by creating dependencies, failing to cultivate individual creativity, and failing to address the spiritual issues a person might have.

3. What are the effects of government welfare? Why?
   a. *Government welfare creates a dependency on the state. This is because those who are receiving services from the state are not given the opportunity to work or to transition out of the aid.*
   b. *Government welfare also reduces work ethic, as people find the more hours they work the less benefit they receive.*

4. What is the biblical role of the state?

   The biblical role of the state according to Moreland is to, "preserve a stable, peaceful social order by punishing wrongdoing that involves the violation of people's negative rights…the state is to be responsible under the Natural Moral Law."

5. How does government spending distort the economy? What effect does it have on private individuals and their decision-making abilities?
   a. *Government spending artificially restricts economic activity through regulations, poor policies, bailouts, etc.*
   b. *These actions distort the market, making it more difficult for private citizens to determine real prices. This results in losses to the economy.*

MODULE 15: GOVERNMENT AND UNINTENDED CONSEQUENCES

1. Is it possible for the government to ration goods based on needs? Why or why not?
   a. *The government has a difficult time rationing resources based on needs because it does not always understand them.*
   b. *The government suffers from the knowledge problem.*
   c. *There is no incentive for the government to make the most of its resources because the government does not operate based on profits and losses.*

2. Are government subsidies given to farmers because certain crops are so expensive to grow, or are certain crops so expensive to grow because the government offers price supports?

   Certain crops are becoming more expensive to grow because the government offers price supports. These supports reduce the competitive pressures to make products and crops better and cheaper.

3. According to Bastiat, what is the triple hypothesis?

   According to Bastiat, the triple hypothesis is "the total inertness of mankind, the omnipotence of the law, and the infallibility of the legislator. These three ideas form the sacred symbol of those who proclaim themselves totally democratic."

4. How does the law get misused as a tool for empowering special interests?
   a. *Those who are in control use the law to benefit themselves at the expense of others by rigging the law in their favor.*
   b. *According to Bastiat, "they do not abolish legal plunder."*

5. Discuss the unintended consequences of the minimum wage in light of the true effects of redistribution we studied last week. How is this different from the free-market outcome?
   a. *Minimum wage laws disrupt the natural market process by acting as a price floor (a government mandated minimum allowed price).*
   b. *Because a price floor is not a form of wealth creation but rather wealth redistribution, price floors create new costs that cause employers to have to either let people go or raise prices.*
   c. *This ends up hurting the people the government was originally trying to help.*

6. Why can't we just wait for the government to provide goods and services? Where does the government get its resources?

   The government receives it resources from taxing the people, and thus there are winners and losers when the government provides goods and services to consumers because we all have differing subjective values. Think of public education, which is coerced through taxation. Not everyone wants it, and most do not benefit as much as they could if the services were privately provided.

MODULE 16: FINAL REFLECTIONS

MIDTERM ANSWER KEY

INSTRUCTIONS

Choose no more than 10 questions for each student to answer. Students should be able to answer each question in about one paragraph and should refer to the ideas covered below.

1. When do we see trade take place in Genesis? Are we created to serve each other through our gifts?
    a. *We see the potential for trade in our creation. We are all created differently, which means we are good at some things relative to others. This was true for Adam and Eve, and it suggests that they worked on different things. Cain and Abel are a good example. Cain raised flocks and Abel worked the soil. They had different skills and likely traded with each other. This does not always imply monetary exchange but certainly barter, which is a form of trade. As more people enter society, more trade takes place.*
    b. *We are created to cultivate God's good creation. We do this by using our creativity and applying it to the world to find better ways of doing things and to solve problems. We cannot do it all on our own because we are limited in our gifts. We are best able to serve one another when we use our gifts and improve them.*

2. What does it mean to think like an economist?
    a. *Thinking like an economist means that we always count the costs of our decisions; we know that nothing is free. Even if there is no monetary price on a good or service, we must surrender our time to have it, and this presents a cost. Not only must we understand costs, but we must weigh the cost with the expected benefit to us.*
    b. *Thinking like an economist also implies that we know we are limited and thus should not try to do everything on our own. Instead, we are better off when we can trade with others based on our skills. We also must look at the long run and assess what the consequences of our choices are, not just in the present time but also in the future. Incentives matter for choices, and if we want to redirect the behavior of others, we must understand their incentives.*

3. What is a free-market economy? Which institutions are involved in a free-market economy? What is the outcome of trade?
    a. *A free-market economy is one in which the market process emerges from individual exchange and is not burdened by excessive regulations and rules that limit the choices and economic exchanges of people.*

    b. *This works well when we have the institutions of well-protected and well-defined property rights within the rule of law. It occurs when people are allowed to open and operate businesses, which in turn fosters creative entrepreneurship.*

    c. *Trade begets more trade, and it increases overall wealth and fosters the productive use of human capital. It fosters creativity and problem solving.*

4. Does anyone know how to make a pencil? Why does this matter?

    a. *No one person knows how to make a pencil. The pencil happens because hundreds of thousands of strangers are knowingly and unknowingly part of the process. The CEO of the pencil company knows what is involved in pencils but does not know how to fell the wood from the forest, how to prepare the coffee that the loggers drink, and how to make the yellow paint that coats the pencil.*

    b. *There are many people involved in the pencil process without knowing what role they play. This is good because if they had to know everything, which no one can, we would not have pencils.*

5. What about our human nature makes interdependence and trading important? Can we flourish alone? Why can't we divide all resources equally?

    a. *We are limited in what we can do and accomplish. God created us to do some things well, but there are many things we do not know how to do. We need each other because the things that we cannot do well, others can do well, and vice versa. The only way for us to benefit from each other's skills is to trade. This trade frees us from figuring out everything on our own and gifts us more time to do what God has created us to do.*

    b. *For these reasons, we cannot flourish if we are left to our own devices. We are finite, and we lack the knowledge we would need to do it all alone. We must be able to rely on the talents of others if we are to flourish.*

    c. *We cannot divide resources equally because that would not help us do what God asks us to do, which is to be creative and serve others. Making our material possessions equal does not make us productive. What makes us productive is living into who God has created us to be with excellence and trading our skills with others through the workplace.*

6. How and why does division of labor make sense biblically and economically? What are the advantages of division of labor for the individual and for society?

    a. *The division of labor is an extension of how we are created uniquely. We are unique and limited, which means that we have something special to offer others but we can't offer everything. We can't do all things well. The division of labor occurs when we all can focus on improving and cultivating our gifts. For example, in car manufacturing no one person assembles or makes an entire car. Different people make different parts; it would be too difficult and expensive to make an entire car alone. In fact, we likely would have very few cars if this were the case. Dividing the labor based on skill means making cars is easier and cheaper, and we get more of them for sale.*

b. *This process makes our labor less frustrating and more fulfilling because we can focus on what we are relatively better at doing. It is better for society because we have more goods and services available for everyone, and this increases opportunities for people to access goods and services, like cars, that save their time and free them to do more things.*

7. How can we think of biblical stewardship within the context of economics?
   Biblical stewardship means that we must use the limited gifts we have to serve God and his creation. Biblical stewardship is about serving others, neighbor and stranger alike. This applies directly to the economic way of thinking—if we want a flourishing society, we must live by these principles. We can only serve others well when we realize that we must have trade so that we can offer our gifts to others and benefit from their gifts.

8. Why do we need incentives to make decisions? Can't we just rely on altruism?
   a. *We all have unique subjective values. Some people like pizza; some do not. These preferences motivate or incentivize the economic choices that people make. If we want people to choose in a certain way, we must understand what motivates them and that subjective value is different for every person.*
   b. *We can't rely on altruism because we are motivated by our self-interest. This is how God created us. Even when we do something nice for someone without asking for anything in return, we still feel good about it, which is getting something in return. Altruism is not a motivating factor on which we can run societies. We need a system that encourages others through good incentives to serve strangers. This happens when we have profits, prices, and property rights.*

9. What can we tell about demand from the supply curve? Why?
   a. *Supply is demand in disguise. We know that supply never exists on its own. Instead, people open businesses and sell things because they think there is a consumer demand for them. Suppliers work hard to serve demanders by trying to understand what it is they want. This fosters entrepreneurship.*
   b. *Supply that exists with no demand will not result in any profit. Very few people, if any, will purchase from you if you create something that is not based on demand.*

10. Can suppliers sell their goods and services at any price they want? Explain.
    If I list my house for sale or have a lemonade stand on the weekend, I can set any price that I want. But because supply must respond to demand, I cannot necessarily sell the items at any price. I may want to charge $100 for each cup of lemonade, but if I want to sell any, I will have to lower my price because most people do not value a cup of lemonade at $100. Suppliers have to serve their customers both in terms of the products they sell and the price consumers are willing to pay.

11. Will technology ever eliminate scarcity? How does our call to creativity help reduce scarcity and increase options?
    a. *We will never eliminate scarcity in this life. We each only have twenty-four hours in a day, and we don't know how many days we have. In this regard, you are very similar to someone who is quite wealthy, like Bill Gates. He may be very rich, but he only has twenty-four hours in each day. It behooves each of us to steward our time well and be as productive as we can with the limited resources we have.*
    b. *When we use our gifts to serve others, we are solving problems and finding new ways to do things. The dishwasher frees me to spend less time cleaning up after dinner. The washing machine allows me to spend less time getting clothes clean, and the car allows me to get places faster than walking. These inventions help us economize our time and free us to do more things in every day. When I have more ways to save time, I have more free time and can use my creative gifts more than I otherwise could.*

12. What are some things that can shift the supply curve?
    An increase or decrease in taxes; changes in resource or input prices, new suppliers entering or leaving the market, or expectations about the future of that market.

13. Delineate the importance of prices, trade, and resource allocation. How are prices set in the free market?
    a. *Prices emerge through individual exchange, and they allow us to understand how much we have to give up to get what we want. Prices help us to best allocate our scarce resources because they give us a mechanism by which to rank the value we place on things. When we can rank value, we are better positioned to know how and when to trade.*
    b. *Prices in a free market are not set by anyone but rather are always changing and evolving based on the changing conditions of the market and the changing desires of consumers.*

14. If prices are emergent and based on scarcity, how will we ever know if a price is "too high"?
    The only way to know if a price is "too high" would be if we observed a price set for which no one made a purchase. If consumers are making purchases, then the price is not "too high." This does not mean that consumers would not like to pay less. We always like to pay less and sellers always like to charge more, but it is the ongoing negotiation between sellers and buyers that results in the prices we see in any given situation, whether the prices of gasoline after a hurricane or the price of a latte at Starbucks.

15. What is the function of profits? Of losses? What would happen if we didn't have them?
    a. *Profits and losses are signals in a free-market economy from consumers to sellers. If a seller earns a profit or has leftover income, then the consumers have given them the feedback that they like*

what is being offered. When iPads first went on the market, Apple ran out of them because consumers liked them so much. This sent a signal to Apple to open more factories and produce more iPads.

  b. *If a seller brings a good or service to the market and it is not what consumers want or it is not a price they are willing to pay, the seller will incur a loss. This loss gives a signal to the seller to change the way they are doing things or to do something entirely different. In this way, losses are very important because they help ensure we are using our scarce resources as productively as possible.*

  c. *If we did not have profits and losses, we would not know what consumers want or how to change based on their changing needs. We would not be able to be good stewards with our skills and time because we would have no feedback from the economy.*

16. How can we think about biblical flourishing and economic progress? Can those things coexist?
They necessarily go together. Economic progress in a free-market society is generally a sign that we are helping improve the lives of others by providing them with goods and services they cannot provide themselves. When our time is freed because we don't have to grow all of our own food, sew all of our own clothes, and provide our own healthcare, we have more time to do what God wants us to and lots of options from which to choose.

17. What is the role of market trade in resource allocation? How does the free market incentivize people to supply goods and services to each other?
Economic exchange that occurs through trade allows us to better allocate scarce resources. Scarce resources can be put to many uses. The wood that comes from trees can make tables, printer paper, toilet paper, and thousands of other items. Economic exchange and the emergence of prices help give signals to producers about how many tables rolls of toilet paper to make, and in a productive society, we get to have both items! In this way, the market uses price signals to tell suppliers what to do and what consumers want. This provides incentives for us to offer the things that people need the most.

18. Explain the difference between greed and self-interest. Is it unbiblical to act out of self-interest? What is the role of self-interest in market trade?

  a. *Self-interest is the way we choose among many alternatives. How do you decide what to have for breakfast? There are many choices in your pantry: eggs, yogurt, oatmeal, or a granola bar. They all fuel your body, so the way you choose is based on what you think will satisfy your needs and desires at the best and the lowest cost. Self-interest is also about sacrifice. I brush my teeth not because it is fun, but because it is good for my long-term health. Entrepreneurs invest their income into their companies because they want to make long-term profits. Self-interest, when our choices are Christ-centered, always involves doing good. When our desires take over, they lead to frustration.*

b. *In free-market trade, our self-interest is the incentive we have to create and to invent new goods and services. Sellers desire profit, and in a free-market they have to earn that profit by being creative and effective. In market trade, self-interest is the best mechanism by which we can encourage strangers to serve each other, and it generates a more peaceful and cooperative society.*

19. What happens when prices are artificially set by something or someone who is not a market participant, such as a law or central planner? Why is this the result?

    The central planner, like the rest of us, has a knowledge problem. They do not know how to set prices because prices are not set from the top down. They emerge from the bottom up, from the repeated exchanges between buyers and sellers. Central planners might know what they want produced, but they have no way to know the right quantity or the right price because this information is only revealed through the process of economic exchange.

20. If scarcity necessitates a rationing mechanism, why is competition beneficial?

    We must ration our resources because we live in a world of scarcity. When sellers compete to serve buyers with things like cars, cell phones, and medicines, we get more of these things and they become both better in quality and cheaper over time. This means that more people have access to these things, which frees them to use their gifts in more productive ways.

21. How does demand for high-tech cell phones in the United States encourage cell phone use in third-world countries?

    The continuing development of cell phone technologies through market competition makes those technologies cheaper and more accessible to lower income groups. Cell phone use in the developing world is providing immense opportunities for women to start small businesses, for workers to be more productive, and in general it gives people a fixed identity.

22. See the chart below. For each "market", draw a supply and demand curve and label the equilibrium price and quantity. Then, graph what happens to that original market after the stated event and mark the new equilibrium. Discuss the results and how they impact our lives. How is each different?

MARKET	EVENT
Gasoline	Hurricane Katrina
Lemons	Frost destroys half the nation's crops
Margarine	There is a decrease in the price of butter
Peanut Butter	Increase in the price of all jellies
Cars	Decrease in the price of subway rides

KEY					
P	Price	Q1	Original Equilibrium Quantity	D1	Original Demand
Q	Quantity	Q2	New Equilibrium Quantity	D2	New Demand
P1	Original Equilibrium Price	S1	Original Supply		
P2	New Equilibrium Price	S2	New Supply		

MARKET & EVENT

1. Gasoline & Hurricane Katrina

After Hurricane Katrina, less crude oil was available to refine into gasoline. This represents a large shock, or decrease, in supply. The supply curve moves back and to the left. As a result, there is less quantity available in the market and prices rise.

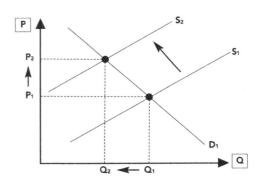

2. Lemons & Frost destroys half the nation's crops

A frost destroys half of the nation's lemons, resulting in a large decrease or negative supply shock. This will cause the supply curve to move back and to the left. This results in less quantity, fewer lemons available for purchase, and higher prices for lemons.

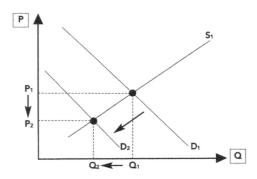

3. Margarine & A decrease in the price of butter

Margarine and butter are substitute goods, meaning one can be used in place of the other. When the price of butter decreases, it means the demand for margarine will decrease or go down. Less margarine will be purchased, and the price will drop as people switch into the market for butter.

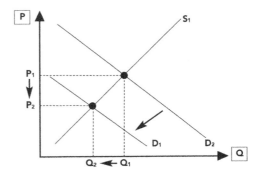

4. Peanut Butter & An increase in the price of all jellies

If peanut butter and jelly are complement goods, meaning they are used together, then people will buy less peanut butter when the price for jelly increases (all else held equal). The demand for peanut butter will decrease, resulting in less peanut butter being purchased and lower peanut butter prices.

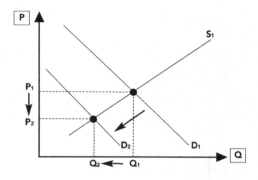

---

5. Cars & A decrease in the price of subway rides

If subway rides and car rides are substitute goods, then there will be a decreased demand for car rides when the price of a subway ride decreases. This causes the demand curve to move down, and there will be fewer car rides taken and lower prices for those that are.

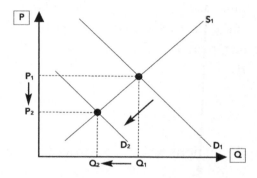

If trade is voluntary, then both parties are better off at the moment of trade because they willingly gave up some of their resources to obtain a good or service. This is driven by subjective value, which motivates our self-interest and our purposeful choices. The policy implication of this is that we don't want to get in the way of or limit voluntary trade if at all possible. When we limit trade, or when the state orchestrates who can trade with whom, we enter a world of zero-sum or negative-sum games where there are winners and losers rather than winners on both sides.

FINAL EXAM ANSWER KEY

MULTIPLE CHOICE QUESTIONS

(CORRECT ANSWER IN BOLD)

1. Which of the following is true?
   a. Scarcity and poverty are the same thing.
   b. **Poverty means that some basic need of a person is not being met.**
   c. Scarcity is the result of price gouging.
   d. All of the above are true.

2. Economics is the study of
   a. How to become a good entrepreneur.
   b. How to make money in the stock market.
   c. How the morals and values of people are formed.
   d. **How individuals make choices under conditions of scarcity.**

3. Which of the following is consistent with the basic economic postulate that incentives matter?
   a. Consumers buy fewer cars when the price of cars rises.
   b. Farmers produce less corn when corn prices decline.
   c. A politician votes for a subsidy when it is in the best interest of a special interest group within his district even if it might harm other voters.
   d. **All of the above.**

4. The highest valued alternative that has to be given up in order to choose an action is called
   a. Scarcity
   b. Absolute value
   c. **Opportunity cost**
   d. Sunk cost

5. Which of the following is not scarce?
   a. Time
   b. Money
   c. Pencils
   d. **Air**
   e. None of the above

6. The law of comparative advantage suggests that
   a. **Individuals, nations, and states can all benefit if they trade with others.**
   b. Free trade among nations harms economies.
   c. Every person and economy should strive to be self-sufficient.
   d. Each person should try to produce as much at home as they can.

7. Private property rights exist when property rights are
   a. Transferrable to others
   b. Protected legally
   c. Exclusively controlled by the owners
   d. **All of the above**

8. Which of the following would allow the production-possibilities frontier for an economy to shift outward?
   a. Better institutions and governance, like converting from socialism to a market-based society.
   b. An increase in the labor force or resources.
   c. More investment which results in better technology.
   d. **All of the above**
   e. None of the above

9. The owners of private property will
   a. Use their property for selfish ends, taking no account of the impact their behavior has on others.
   b. **Use their property in ways that others value because the market will generally reward them for it.**
   c. Engage in poor environmental stewardship.
   d. Lose profits when they take the wishes of others into consideration.

10. When Benjamin Franklin wrote "Remember that Time is Money!" he understood
    a. That property rights create incentives.
    b. The law of comparative advantage.
    c. Biblical stewardship.
    d. **The concept of opportunity cost.**

TRUE/FALSE
(WITH EXPLANATION)

Please write a two- to three-sentence explanation for your answer:

1. In each trade, there is a winner and a loser. Voluntary trade cannot make both parties better off.
   (False) *When trade is voluntary and there is no coercion to purchase, both parties are better off than they were before. Voluntary trade always makes both parties better off, and this is based on our choices predicated on our subjective values and self-interest.*

2. Property that is privately owned tends to be better cared for and better preserved than property that is not privately owned.
   (True) *When a person owns their property and can be assured that they get to keep it, they then have an incentive to take care of it and make investments in it. This keeps valuable resources sustainable and ensures that we don't deplete them.*

3. Consumers will purchase fewer hamburgers at higher prices than at lower prices if other factors remain the same.
   (True) *When the price of a good or service that we like increases, we will naturally want less of it. If there are many substitutes for that good, as there are for hamburgers, then people will quickly stop eating hamburgers and perhaps start consuming hot dogs or another substitute good.*

4. An increase in the demand for coffee would cause its price to rise and producers to expand output.
   (True) *When the demand for something increases, in the short term, the price will increase because we are putting pressure on a scarce resource that we cannot make more of overnight. In the longer run, coffee growers will plant more trees and harvest more beans, which means there will be more available for more consumers and the price will tend to go back down.*

5. The law of supply reflects the willingness of producers to expand output in response to an increase in the price of a product.
   (True) *Suppliers need an incentive to offer their goods and services to customers. Price is their incentive, and as the price they can garner increases, they will offer more to the market. Think about if you open a lemonade stand and are able to get $5 per glass rather than $.50 per glass. You would make more lemonade and stay outside all day, because the price provides you a renewed and stronger incentive to do so.)*

ESSAY QUESTIONS

(CHOOSE SIX)

These should take three to four paragraphs to answer. No answers are listed because these are meant to be open-ended questions.

1. Discuss how our own call to work in Genesis necessitates that we use the economic way of thinking when we make decisions.

2. Discuss how the article "I, Pencil" demonstrates that market economies bring us into community with one another.

3. Talk about how the Hayek reading "The Use of Knowledge in Society" relates to the reading "I, Pencil."

4. What do prices do in a market setting? Discuss specifically how they operate as signaling devices.

5. List the five components of economic freedom. Which is most in jeopardy in the United States today and why?

6. What does doing our jobs well, as God has called us to, have to do with helping the poor?

7. Why does market trade result in higher levels of prosperity?

8. What is the most important lesson you have learned about economics in this class, and how will it change your outlook in the future?

GRAPH SHIFTING

1. In the market for motorcycles, what happens when the wages of motorcycle workers decreases?

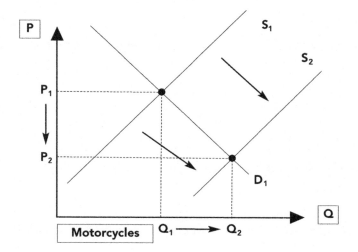

When the workers who make motorcycles become cheaper to employ, the firms will hire more of them because an input into their production process has become less scarce relative to other inputs. This means the supply curve will shift to the right, which is an increase in supply. The new equilibrium price of motorcycles will be lower, and more will be sold. In this regard, more consumers will have access to them. Make sure your child marks the new equilibrium price and quantity. This shows how the overall market has changed as a result of that input price changing.

2. In the market for lemons, what happens when a frost destroys half of the lemons in Florida?

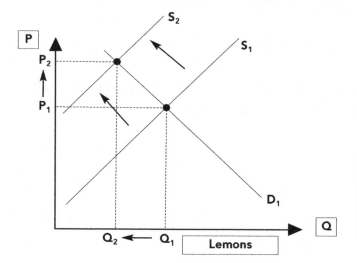

When we lose a resource due to a natural disaster or weather occurrence, the supply will decrease, and the curve will shift to the left. The new equilibrium price will be higher, and fewer lemons will be available than would be without the frost. These types of events are bad for prosperity because fewer people will have access to this good. This could happen with services too. Prosperity means that more is available for less over time and these types of events harm that and make fewer goods and services available for consumers. Make sure to have your child mark the new price and quantity.

3. If peanut butter and jelly are complement goods, what happens to the jelly market when peanut butter becomes cheaper?

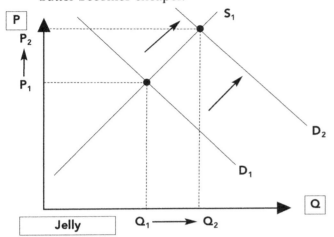

If goods are complementary, that means they are often consumed together (remember this is all predicated on the subjective value of the consumer). For this consumer, when peanut butter becomes cheaper (i.e., more plentiful), then we will see the people who consume these products together buy more jelly to accompany their peanut butter. This means the demand curve for jelly will shift up (an increase), and the resulting price will be higher and more will be purchased.

4. In the market for smartphones, what happens if there is a decrease in Economic Freedom and everyone's incomes decline?

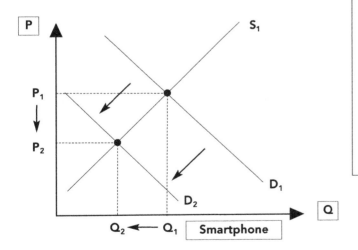

If everyone has less money to spend because of a drop in income and prosperity, demand for goods like smartphones can decline. This would result in a negative shift (down and to the left), which would result in a lower price and fewer sold. When people have less money to spend on the things they want, the result will be that there are more available than people desire, which will result in a decrease in price. Make sure to have your child mark the new equilibrium price and quantity.

5. If Blu-ray players become cheaper, what happens in the market for DVD players?

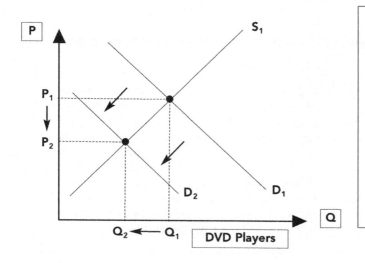

When a good that has a close substitute (i.e., something that can be used in lieu of something else), then the market for both goods will be affected. As new technology emerges and makes Blu-ray players better and cheaper than DVD players, people will switch from consuming (purchasing) the DVD to consuming the Blu-Ray, which means the demand for the outdated DVD player will decrease (a negative shift in the curve, which is a shift downward and to the left). This will result in a lower price and fewer DVD players purchased. Make sure your child marks the new equilibrium price and quantity.

Price	Initial Quantity Demanded	Quantity Supplied	New Quantity Demanded
$2	60	20	80
$4	50	30	70
$6	40	40	60
$8	30	50	50
$10	20	60	40

6. See the chart above and graph the following:
    a. The initial demand curve
    b. The initial supply curve
    c. What is the equilibrium price?
    d. The area experiences much economic progress and everyone wants more. See the "New Quantity Demanded" column and graph it.
    e. What is the new equilibrium price?
    f. Has demand changed or is this a change in quantity demanded?

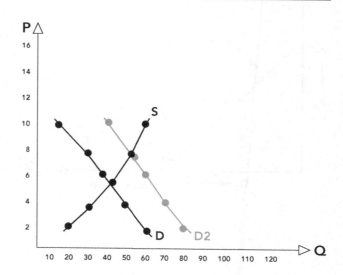

ABOUT THE INSTITUTE FOR FAITH, WORK & ECONOMICS

The Institute for Faith, Work & Economics™ (IFWE) is a nonprofit, 501(c)(3) Christian research organization committed to promoting biblical and economic principles that help individuals find fulfillment in their work and contribute to a free and flourishing society. IFWE's research starts with the belief that the Bible, as the inerrant Word of God, provides the authoritative and intellectual foundation for a proper understanding of work and economic truths that, when properly followed, can help individuals, companies, communities, and nations flourish.

IFWE's research is based on three core principles:

- Each person is created in God's image and, like him, has a desire to be creative and to find **fulfillment** using their God-given talents through work.

- All work, whether paid or volunteer, matters to God, and we as Christians are called to pursue excellence throughout the week—not just on Sundays—stewarding all that we've been given for God's glory and for the **flourishing** of society.

- Therefore, we as citizens must promote an economic environment that not only provides us the **freedom** to pursue our callings and flourish in our work but also reflects the inherent dignity of every human being.

Our desire is to help Christians view their work within the bigger picture of what God is doing in the world. Not only do we help Christians find personal fulfillment, but we also help them understand how to better alleviate poverty, address greed, and view possessions properly. With a biblical view of work and economics, we can partner together to be meaningful participants in God's plan to restore the world to the way he intended it to be.

START HERE

The Institute for Faith, Work & Economics provides many resources to help you live a life of freedom, fulfillment, and flourishing. These tools are designed to fit into your life and provide biblical encouragement and guidance to your walk with God.

BLOG
Get our daily or weekly blog updates in your inbox.
BLOG.TIFWE.ORG

RESEARCH
Download free in-depth studies to further your understanding of faith, work, and economics.
RESEARCH.TIFWE.ORG

SOCIALIZE
Connect with IFWE on social media and join the conversation.
FACEBOOK.COM / FAITHWORKECON
TWITTER.COM / FAITHWORKECON

BOOK STORE
Get our latest releases and educational products.
STORE.TIFWE.ORG

DONATE
Become a partner in bringing about flourishing.
DONATE.TIFWE.ORG

PARTICIPATE
Find information about student groups, upcoming events, and other opportunities to get involved.
CONNECT.TIFWE.ORG

Made in the USA
Monee, IL
11 August 2025

23068280R00033